Piano • Vocal • Guitar

Best of Sly & the Family Stone

16 Soul Classics

Cover photo © Photofest

ISBN 978-1-4768-1290-8

HAL•LEONARD®
CORPORATION

7777 W. BLUEMOUND RD. P.O. BOX 13819 MILWAUKEE, WI 53213

Visit Hal Leonard Online at
www.halleonard.com

DANCE TO THE MUSIC

Words and Music by
SYLVESTER STEWART

I'm gon-na add a lit-tle gui - tar and make it eas - y to move your feet.

I'm gon-na add some bot - tom so that the

EVERYBODY IS A STAR

Words and Music by
SYLVESTER STEWART

EVERYDAY PEOPLE

Words and Music by
SYLVESTER STEWART

Moderate Pop feel

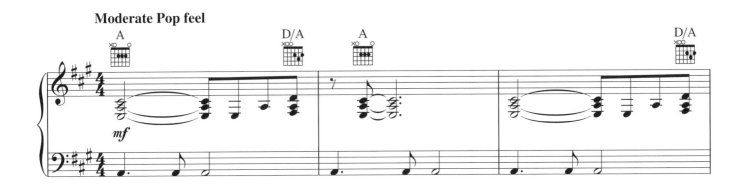

Some-times I'm right, and I can be wrong. ___
I'm no bet - ter and nei - ther are you. ___

My own be - liefs ___ are in my songs. ___ The butch - er, the bank - er, the
We're all the same, ___ what - ev - er you do. ___ You love me, you hate me, you

FAMILY AFFAIR

Words and Music by
SYLVESTER STEWART

Moderately

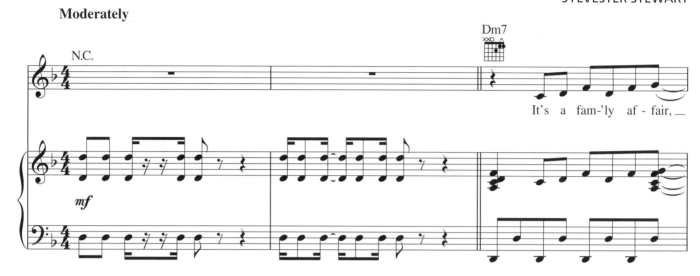

It's a fam-'ly af - fair,

it's a fam-'ly af-fair. _____

It's a fam-'ly af - fair, _____ it's a fam-'ly af - fair. _

New - ly - wed _____ a year a-

HOT FUN IN THE SUMMERTIME

Words and Music by
SYLVESTER STEWART

I WANT TO TAKE YOU HIGHER

Words and Music by
SYLVESTER STEWART

Medium Rock

I wan-na take you high - er.
Don't ya wan-na get high - er?
Wan-na take you high - er.

Ba - by, ba - by, ba - by, light my fire.

To Coda

I wan-na take you high - er.

N.C.

Boom lak - a - lak - a - lak - a, boom lak - a - lak - goon - ka boom.

(high - er.) Do you wan-na go (High - er.) With me, me,

(High - er.) and you, you. (High - er.) Won't ya light my fire? _ Woo, yeah!

Wan-na take you high - er. _

A7

Boom lak - a - lak - a - lak - a, boom lak - a - lak - a - lak - a, boom lak - a - lak - a - lak - a, boom lak - a - lak - a - lak - a,

Instrumental solo

boom lak - a - lak - a - lak - a, boom lak - a - lak - a - lak - a, boom lak - a - lak - a - lak - a, boom lak - a - lak - a - lak - a.

(High - er.) Do you feel it? (High - er.) Yeah...

Don't you wan - na go

high - er? ___ Woo! I wan-na take you high - er. Yeah, yeah.

IF YOU WANT ME TO STAY

Words and Music by
SYLVESTER STEWART

* Recorded a half step higher.

see me a - gain, ___ I hope you have been ___ the kind of per - son you real - ly are now. I'll ___ be ___ so good. I wish I could _ get the mes - sage o - ver to you now. ___

Repeat and Fade

LUV N' HAIGHT

Words and Music by
SYLVESTER STEWART

Medium Funk

* Recorded a half step higher.

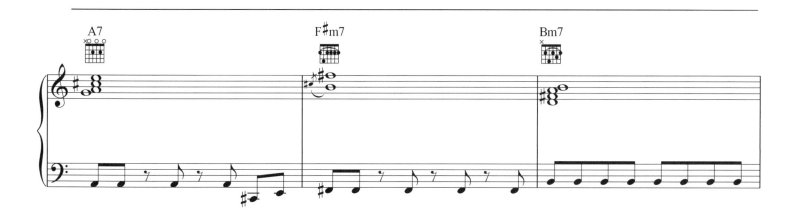

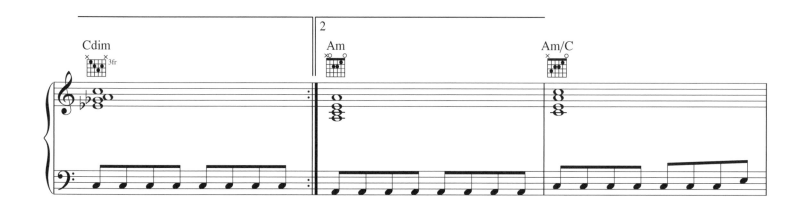

RUNNIN' AWAY

Words and Music by
SYLVESTER STEWART

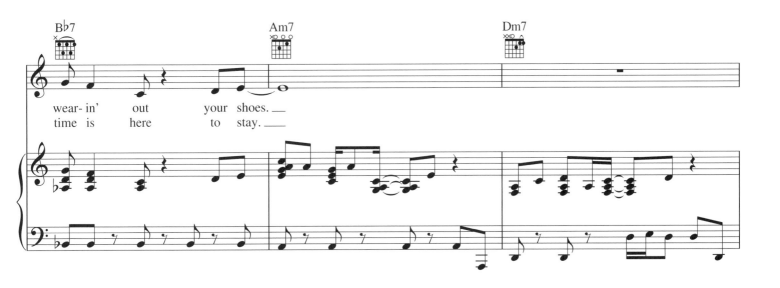

* Recorded a half step higher.

POET

Words and Music by
SYLVESTER STEWART

Medium Funk

My on-ly weap-on is my pen, _____ yeah,

and the frame of mind I'm in, _____ yeah. I'm a song-writ-er.

Well, well, well, a po-et. I'm a song-writ-er,

SING A SIMPLE SONG

Words and Music by
SYLVESTER STEWART

D.S. al Coda

CODA

ya   ya._____   Sing__ it in__ the show - er._____

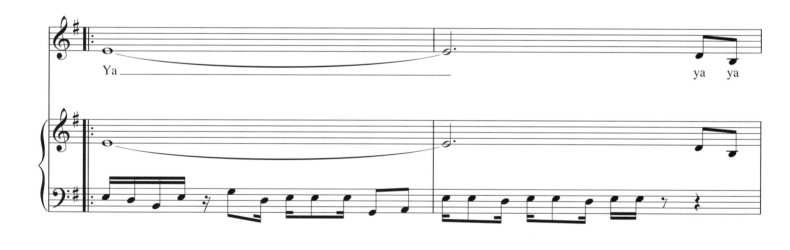

Ya _____   ya   ya

Repeat ad lib. and Fade

ya   ya._____

(You Caught Me)
SMILIN'

Words and Music by
SYLVESTER STEWART

58

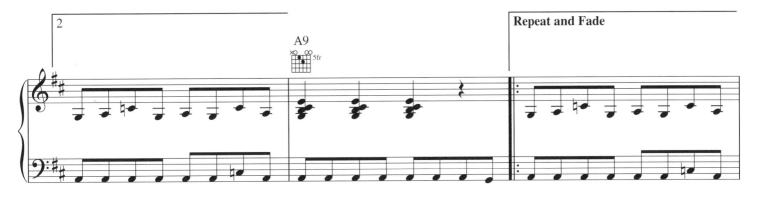

You caught me

Repeat and Fade

Optional Ending

STAND!

Words and Music by
SYLVESTER STEWART

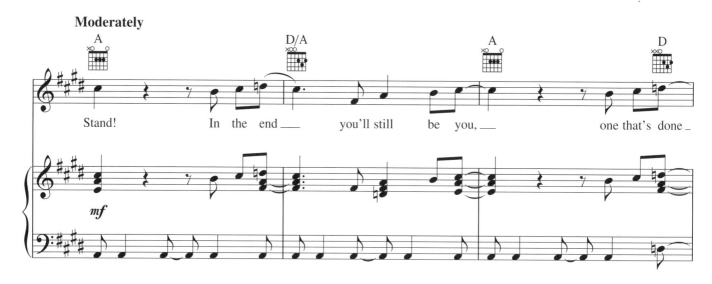

Stand! In the end ___ you'll still be you, ___ one that's done ___

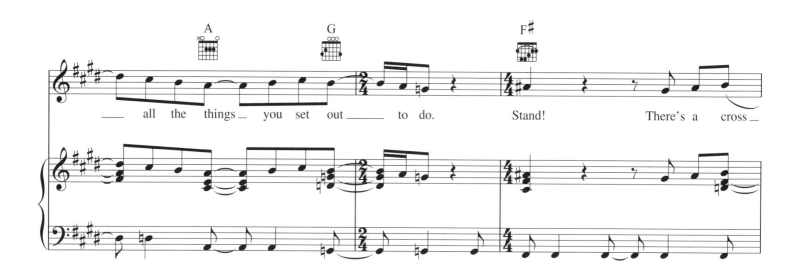

___ all the things ___ you set out ___ to do. Stand! There's a cross ___

___ for you to bear, ___ things to go ___ through if you're ___ go-in' an-

THANK YOU
(Falletinme Be Mice Elf Again)

Words and Music by
SYLVESTER STEWART

66

Flam - ing eyes __ of peo - ple fear __ burn - ing in - to you.

Man - y men __ are miss - ing much, __ hat - ing what they do.

Youth and truth __ are mak - ing love: __ dig it for a start - er now.

Dy - ing young __ is hard to take; sell - ing out is hard - er.

UNDERDOG

Words and Music by
SYLVESTER STEWART

1. I know how it feels__ to ex-pect to get__ a fair shake. But they won't let__ you for-get __'cause you're an

2., 3. (See additional lyrics)

un - der-dog and you've got to be twice__ as good. Yeah, yeah.

Additional Lyrics

2. I know how it feels to get demoted
   When it comes time to get promoted.
   But you might be movin' up too fast, yeah.
   (Yeah, yeah)

   If you ever loved somebody of a different set,
   I bet the set didn't let you forget
   That it just don't go like that.
   (Yeah, yeah)

   I know how it feels for people to stop,
   Turn around and stare,
   Signify a lil' bit of low life, don't rate me, yeah.
   (Yeah, yeah)
   I don't mind.

   I'm the underdog,
   No, I can handle it.
   I'm the underdog,
   I'm the underdog, yeah.
   Underdog.

3. I know how it feels to be played a pawn,
   To be at the party but you're really…
   You're really all alone.
   (Yeah, yeah)
   But just underestimate me.

   I know how it feels when you're feelin' down
   And you wanna come up,
   But you feel like you're in the wrong part of town.
   (Yeah, yeah)

   I know how it feels to have to go along with people
   You don't even know,
   Simply because it happens to be a whole lot more bill.
   (Yeah, yeah)

   Said I'm the underdog.
   I'm the underdog,
   I don't mind, I can handle it.
   Underdog.
   It's gonna be alright,
   I'm the underdog.

YOU CAN MAKE IT IF YOU TRY

Words and Music by
SYLVESTER STEWART

Don't let the plas - tic bring you down. _____
Wake up and go for what you know. _____

Yeah, yeah, yeah, yeah, yeah, yeah. yeah, yeah, yeah.

You can make it if you try. _____ You can make it if you

try. _____

You get what's due _____ you, _____
Time still _____ creep - in' _____

ev-'ry-thing com-in' to you. _ You got to move if you want to be a - head. _
'spec - ially when you're sleep - in'. _ Wake up and go _ for _ what you know. _

You can make it if you try. _____

You can make it if you

try. _____

You can make it if you try. _____

Repeat and Fade

You can make it if you try. _____